GEORGE RUSSELL (AE)	Richard M. Kain and James H. O'Brien
IRIS MURDOCH	Donna Gerstenberger
MARY LAVIN	Zack Bowen
FRANK O'CONNOR	James H. Matthews
ELIZABETH BOWEN	Edwin J. Kenney, Jr.
WILLIAM ALLINGHAM	Alan Warner
SEAMUS HEANEY	Robert Buttel
THOMAS DAVIS	Eileen Sullivan

SEAMUS HEANEY

Robert Buttel

Lewisburg
BUCKNELL UNIVERSITY PRESS
London: Associated University Presses

821.91   H4343bu

Associated University Presses, Inc.
Cranbury, New Jersey 08512

Associated University Presses
108 New Bond Street
London W1Y OQX, England

Library of Congress Cataloging in Publication Data

, Buttel Robert.
  Seamus Heaney.

  (The Irish writers series)
  Bibliography: p.
  1. Heaney, Seamus.
  PR6058.E2Z57   821'.9'14   74-3616
  ISBN 0-8387-1567-2
  ISBN 0-8387-1568-0 pbk.

Printed in the United States of America

Contents

7

Chronology

1939:   Born April 13 in townland of Mossbawn,
            near Castledawson, County Derry, to Patrick
            and Margaret Kathleen (née McCann)
            Heaney; eldest of nine children, two sisters
            and six brothers (one now deceased).

1945-51:   Attends the local Anahorish Primary School.

1951-57:   Boarder at St. Columb's College, Derry.

1957-61:   Student at Queen's University, Belfast, re-
            ceiving B.A. in English Language and Litera-
            ture; member of the University Gaelic Soci-
            ety and also of a local dramatic society;
            Master of Ceremonies of the local Céilidhe
            (Irish dancing); writes and publishes poems
            in undergraduate literary magazines.

1961-62:   Takes postgraduate course at St. Joseph's
            College of Education, Andersontown, Bel-
            fast.

1962-63:   Teaching at St. Thomas's Secondary School,
            Ballymurphy, Belfast; "Turkeys Observed"
            published in *Belfast Telegraph*, "Mid-Term
            Break" in *Kilkenny Magazine*, and "Ad-
            vancement of Learning" in the *Irish Times*.

1963-66:   Lecturer in English at St. Joseph's College;
            New Statesman publishes "Digging," "Scaf-
            folding," and "Storm on an Island" in
            December, 1964 (noticed by Faber and
            Faber); associated with Philip Hobsbaum's
            poetry group wherein he meets other young
            poets; begins to review for *New Statesman,
            Listener*, etc.

1965:   *11 Poems* (pamphlet) published by Festival
            Publications, Belfast; married in August to
            Marie Devlin.

1966:   *Death of a Naturalist* published by Faber
            and Faber in May; son, Michael, born in
            July; receives E. C. Gregory Award.

1966-72:   Lecturer in English (Modern Literature) at
            Queen's University, Belfast; begins contri-
            buting to BBC educational broadcasts, radio
            and television.

1968:   Receives Somerset Maugham Award and
            Geoffrey Faber Prize; son, Christopher, born
            in February.

1969:   *Door into the Dark* published by Faber and
            Faber in June; it becomes Poetry Book Soci-
            ety Choice.

1970-71:   Guest Lecturer at University of California,
            Berkeley.

1972:   Moves from Belfast to Ashford, County
            Wicklow; *Wintering Out* published by Faber
            and Faber in November; engaged on transla-
            tion of Middle Irish romance *Buile Shu-
            ibhne.*

1973:   Receives Denis Devlin Award and Writer in

Residence Award from The American Irish
Foundation; daughter, Catherine Ann, born
in April.

Introduction

Sam Thompson, the Ulster playwright, was driven to label Belfast the "Siberia of the Arts"; so Seamus Heaney relates in a 1966 article in the *New Statesman*, "Out of London: Ulster's Troubles," in which he considers the cultural effects of Belfast's political ties with Westminster and its dependence on London for guidance in the arts. Lacking self-sufficiency, the capital is oppressively provincial, a condition exacerbated by the Paisley movement's breaking down of any bridges that might have existed between Catholics and Protestants. Despite this arid cultural climate, Heaney had grounds for saying in his article that he could see signs of a developing indigenous cultural life. In a fine essay on Ulster poetry in a volume he has edited (*Causeway: the Arts in Ulster*, Belfast, 1971) Michael Longley, Heaney's fellow-poet and friend, says that the "progress of Ulster poetry this century has defined itself in a sequence of energetic spurts" and that it "was not until 1965 that the *Festival Publications* series of pamphlets inaugurated a new phase." One of these pamphlets was Heaney's *11 Poems*. Actually, however, this phase really began to materialize a few years before (about 1962, Heaney tells me) when the English poet Philip Hobsbaum became, according to Longley, "a lecturer in English at Queen's University" and "ran a weekly discussion group which several of the new generation of poets attended. At these sessions new work was analysed with Leavisite rigour: the atmosphere was electric. Various talents may certainly have been emerging on their own" but here the process was accelerated. Furthermore, however spasmodic the twentieth-century Ulster tradition in poetry has been, it has offered support for this latest spurt (which may well be more prolonged than the earlier ones). Longley quotes Heaney's comment in a review of the *Collected Poems* of John Hewitt, one of the preceding generation of poets, that Hewitt's "lifelong concern to question and document the relationship between art and locality has provided all subsequent Northern writers with a hinterland of reference, should they require a tradition more intimate than the broad perspectives of the English literary achievement."

In three volumes of poems to date Heaney's contribution to the current renaissance has been outstanding, but his importance outweighs his role in that ongoing event. He is a special instance of a poet who has transcended the limitations of the provincial by being inordinately true to the material of his locality. It is not that his method has remained insulated from those "broad perspectives" from England (or America) but that his central impulses have derived from the "more intimate" Northern Irish tradition. In his introduction to *Causeway* Longley quotes Patrick Kavanagh on the distinction between the provincial and the parochial: a provincial, with "no mind of his own," trusts only "what the metropolis . . . has to say on the subject"; on the other hand, "parochialism is universal; it deals with fundamentals." In this sense Heaney is a parochial poet. With his own sensibility and mind he has dug into the fundamentals of his conscious and unconscious experience, into the mythos of place, the traces of racial memory, the dark human and natural forces, the archetypal patterns, and done so with such urgency that he breaks through the bonds of provincialism. His poems should give pause to those who automatically reject poetry that has its roots in the regional and traditional.

In technique Heaney's poetry would appear to be traditional; and for this reason it is also rejected by some. Outwardly, the forms are traditional; the poet does usually compose in stanzaic patterns, often (though less and less frequently in the three volumes) with set rhyme-schemes. But what goes on within those patterns is very innovative, it seems to me: art and locality relate in a style that is inimitably Heaney's. In "Traditions" (*Wintering Out*) he complains, "Our gutteral muse/ was bulled long ago/ by the alliterative tradition,/ her uvula grows/ vestigial," but we notice that the verbal energy of the complaint is hardly vestigial. If Mallarmé is the poet for whom language attenuates into the condition of music, Heaney is one poet for whom language coalesces into living texture and movement. His poetry is worth serious study for this reason alone.

Heaney must be considered an Irish poet, not just a Northern Irish one, but knowledge of his work is spreading beyond that island and the British Isles. I noticed recently, for example, that five of his poems have been included in the new *Norton Anthology of Modern*

Poetry. For the reader who has not yet discovered his work I would urge that he have beside him as he reads this study copies of Heaney's three volumes since what follows is at least in part a guide to individual poems.

Seamus Heaney

1

Beginnings

"A poet begins involved with craft, with aspirations that are chiefly concerned with making," Seamus Heaney has said in a statement about his aims which he wrote two or three years ago to accompany a selection of his poems (*Corgi Poets in Focus 2*). The poet "needs a way of saying and there is a first language he can learn from the voices of other poets, dead and alive." He could have cited "Turkeys Observed" as an illustration of part of his own apprenticeship; this poem, which appeared in the *Belfast Telegraph* in 1962 (and later in *Death of a Naturalist*), was his first published one aside from several published before then over the pseudonym Incertus in *Gorgon* and *Q*, Queen's University literary magazines. It is not that one detects specific models; rather, the poem seems an exercise in applying some of the standard practices of modern poetry. The poem is characterized by imagistic exactitude: a dead turkey is "A skin bag plumped with inky putty." And it employs a conceit of the sort favored by the Thirties poets: "I find him ranged with his cold squadrons:/ The fuselage is bare, the proud wings snapped,/ The tail-fan stripped down to a shameful rudder" (with the pathos of these concluding lines sunk by the weight of contrivance). Some of the alliteration may be heavy-handed, as in "*B*lue-*b*reasted in their indifferent *m*ortuary,/ *B*eached *b*are on the cold *m*arble sla*b*s/ In i*mm*odest underwear *f*rills of *f*eather"—the apprentice reveling here in the craft of prosody; and the word "cowers" in "a turkey cowers in death" may be excessive, but the poet has carefully maintained the elegiac tone, in the modern way, by the "non-poetic" subject matter, by the objectivity of the title, and by the neutrality of the opening line—"One observes them, one expects them." The controlled movement of the poem also sustains the tone: within the four-line stanzas the rhythms are fluent but firm, and, since evidently no rhyme scheme arose naturally in the genesis of the poem, none was forcibly imposed. Although the turkeys, in the setting of "bleak Christmas dazzle," are surely emblems of mortality, their symbolic import is not overly insisted upon.

Basically this is a well-made poem, an academic exercise in the modern mode, the voice for the most part anonymous, still to be discovered. Only in the graphic force of the line "A skin bag plumped with inky putty" and in the second stanza, particularly in the oxymoron "smelly majesty" with its earthy adjective and in the energy of the phrase describing the inert beef, "A half-cow slung from a hook," does the poem anticipate the poet's distinctive manner:

> The red sides of beef retain
> Some of the smelly majesty of living:
> A half-cow slung from a hook maintains
> That blood and flesh are not ignored.

A very promising apprentice poem, then. Heaney, again in the *Corgi* statement, refers to this stage of a poet's development as "a mimicry and a posturing that leads to confidence, a voice of his own that he begins to hear, prompting behind lines he has learned."

The poet's confidence was emerging rapidly at this time, for "Mid-Term Break," a *Death of a Naturalist* poem, published in *Kilkenny Magazine* not long after the appearance of "Turkeys Observed," indicates how ably he could now apply his new-found craft to a poetic statement concerning a painful personal experience. Heaney says that the poem, an elegy for a young brother killed in an auto accident, came to him quite spontaneously, that it almost wrote itself without his thinking about craft. Only in the prosodic overdetermination of the first two lines (the speaker "sat all morning in the *college sick bay/ Counting bells knelling classes* to a *close*") is there an intrusion of the craftsman at work. The rest reads as a straight recital of the literal details; a litany of trite comforting words becomes part of the quiet testimony of grief: "Big Jim Evans saying it was a hard blow," "And I was embarrassed/ By old men standing up to shake my hand/ And tell me they were 'sorry for my trouble,'" "as my mother held my hand/ In hers and coughed out angry tearless sighs." The lament is undramatized, controlled, simply reported:

> Next morning I went up into the room. Snowdrops
> And candles soothed the bedside; I saw him
> For the first time in six weeks. Paler now,
>
> Wearing a poppy bruise on his left temple,
> He lay in the four foot box as in his cot.
> No gaudy scars, the bumper knocked him clear.

A four foot box, a foot for every year.

The ritual effect of the snowdrops and candles occurs because it was part of the ritual scene; "poppy bruise" is poetically shocking because descriptively accurate; the laconic explanation, "the bumper knocked him clear," and the cruel mathematics of the one-line coda accentuate the understated bitter sadness. The directness, openness, and apparent matter-of-factness in this poem, on a difficult subject for poetry, have become recurrent characteristics of Heaney's voice.

"An Advancement of Learning," however, published in the *Irish Times* following the two previous poems and later in *Death of a Naturalist*, begins to project much more clearly the poet's individual voice. "Here," to quote once again from the *Corgi* statement, "craft passes into technique which is the ability to send the voice in pursuit of the self," and in this poem we follow this very process. If, as Heaney continues, "Technique is dynamic, active, restless, an ever provisional stance of the imagination towards experience," we see here imagination and technique rising to a greater degree of individuality; the poem is definitely in the poet's own idiom though it does exhibit a residue of "mimicry and posturing." The *Times Literary Supplement* reviewer of *Death of a Naturalist,* although finding the volume substantial and impressive, complained that "the most obvious surface fault is the rather glib or incongruous imagery stuck on in what seems to be an attempt to hit the required sophistication," quoting as illustration the first two stanzas of the poem, which concerns an encounter with a rat:

I took the embankment path
(As always, deferring
The bridge). The river nosed past,
Pliable, oil-skinned, wearing

A transfer of gables and sky.
Hunched over the railing,
Well away from the road now, I
Considered the dirty-keeled swans.

For the reviewer " 'nosed' and 'pliable' are surely doubt-
ful; 'oil-skinned' is clever, but introduces an extraneous
association; 'transfer' is somehow uncomfortably neat
and final." I would quibble some with this assess-
ment: "Transfer" is clever, all right, but it does indicate
the observer's indulgence in idle romantic musings, see-
ing a pretty picture on the river surface despite the pollution, and it is not final since the pictorial image is
picked up in the following stanza in the word "smudging," when the observer's reverie is intruded upon by
the obscene reality of a rat which "slobbered curtly,
close,/ Smudging the silence."

But more important than the question of limitations
is the fact that in this early poem Heaney seized upon
an area of subject matter and knowledge congenial to
the discovery of his authentic voice. The vividness of
physical detail in "back bunched and glistening,/ Ears
plastered down on his knobbed skull" and the energy of
word and speech in "But God, another was nimbling/
Up the far bank" and "A rat/ Slimed out of the
water"—with adjective and noun here metamorphosing
into disturbing active verbs: these are typical qualities
in the first volume. One notes too the physical accuracy
of the response in "My throat sickened so quickly that/

I turned down the path in cold sweat," with the repetition of sound in "sickened" and "quickly" an aural counterpart of actual constrictions in the throat. The effect comes naturally, denying thoughts of either craft or technique; here imagination is in full accord with the experience, and the experience occurs with a psychological rightness, moving from sickening shock to "thrilled care" and observation to a control of the situation; yet at the end a subtle balance of ambiguous reactions is struck, with both distaste and sympathy for the creature bound together with a recognition of man's pollution of nature—"This terror, cold, wet-furred, small-clawed,/ Retreated up a pipe for sewage." The discoveries in this poem prepared for the thoroughly distinctive and successful title poem of the collection, "Death of a Naturalist," which I will discuss later.

Heaney's literary and linguistic background was not unusual for a boy brought up on a County Derry farm. Like other children at that time in the environs of Mossbawn, between Castledawson and Toome Bridge, along the Bann River just north of where it emerges from Lough Neagh, about thirty miles northwest of Belfast, he was exposed to the remnants of the oral tradition, the local lore and anecdotes, and the stories brought home from or heard at cattle fairs. He tells me that one of his father's cousins, who might be described as one of the surviving hedgerow "schoolmasters," would visit once a week and read and recite to the children in the family. Occasionally as a young boy and as the eldest child in the family he was called upon at a children's party or when friends and relatives visited to recite verses or sing a song, sentimental or patriotic things,

Michael Dwyer's "Sullivan Beare," say, or "Me Da" by
the Ulster folk poet W. F. Marshall, or a Percy French
ballad such as "The Four Farrellys." Like his fellow
students he received training in Gaelic, an extension of
his linguistic identity and at least an acquaintance with
another and yet a native linguistic tradition. As a boy,
though, he wrote next to no poetry, unless one were to
count the adolescent, roguish Latin verses that he, along
with some his schoolmates at St. Columb's, wrote now
and then for amusement and passed surreptitiously to
one another. Perhaps, however, it is a sign of his future
interest in writing poetry that while at St. Columb's he
did try his hand at composing some Miltonic verses,
though he got no further than three lines. While there he
had one particular advantage, a very good English teacher who had his students reading deeply and thoroughly
in Shakespeare, Chaucer, Wordsworth, and Keats, and
he recalls reading Eliot's "The Hollow Men" at that
time.

At Queen's University Heaney's interests became
more definitely literary. There in the English syllabus he
encountered a wider range of literature, other poets in
the English tradition such as Clare and Hardy (as John
Press in an article in *The Southern Review* has pointed
out) and Hopkins, but also twentieth-century poets. At
the same time he was becoming conscious of the Irish
tradition, Yeats of course and other poets, both Anglo-
Irish and unhyphenated Irish. He remembers reading
Patrick Kavanagh's "The Great Hunger" during this
period, and its powerful effect on him, for it was a
modern poem that suggested possibilities for treating
Irish subject matter. Then, while at St. Joseph's College

of Education in 1961-62, he discovered and read *Six Irish Poets*, edited by Robin Skelton and including Austin Clarke, Richard Kell, Thomas Kinsella, John Montague, Richard Murphy, and Richard Weber. Also he wrote for a course he was taking a long paper on literary magazines in Ulster and learned through this project that a body of poetry could exist outside the classical English canon. Here were Irish poets, what's more Northern Irish poets, who had created a poetry out of their local and native background—W. R. Rodgers and John Hewitt especially. In the latter Heaney found not only a regionalist but one who was also quite urbane. Meanwhile he was continuing to discover other, non-Irish, poets too, R. S. Thomas and Ted Hughes, for example. It was also during this time, while these various influences were contributing to his own interests and urgings and adding to his growing assurance, and while his poems were beginning to be published, that he became one of a group of young writers who met regularly to discuss their work at the home of the English poet Philip Hobsbaum, who had come to teach at Queen's the year Heaney was at St. Joseph's. This was a group, says Heaney, that "generated a literary life" in Belfast; it was in this group that the poet met his friend and fellow poet, Michael Longley. Now he was no longer working in isolation. Here was a "forum" where he received serious criticism which countered the pleasing corroboration he felt when editors began accepting his poems.

The relatively few poems he wrote as an undergraduate dramatize the leap he was to make so shortly afterward. "Reaping in Heat," for example, depends on such poeticisms as "sycamores heaved a sleepless sigh" and "Lark's trills/ Shimmered" and it concludes on a Keatsian-Georgian note:

> . . . Lower
> And deeper and cooler sinks now
> The sycamores' shade, and naked sheaves
> Are whitening on the empty stubble.

"October Thought" shows the impress of Hopkins on the neophyte poet:

> Minute movement millionfold whispers twilight
> Under heaven-hue plum-blue and gorse pricked with gold,
> And through the knuckle-gnarl of branches, poking the night
> Comes the trickling tinkle of bells, well in the fold.

Heaney says that he was captivated by Dylan Thomas's poetry at this time too and published in *Gorgon* or *Q* a poem very much in the Welsh poet's manner (though I have been unable to locate this poem and one or two others). "October Thought" is typical of what any number of university students might produce, though few of them would develop beyond this point. We can see in hindsight, however, that Heaney's obvious imitation of Hopkins (and I suspect that the same could be said of the Thomas poem) was, in its intricate wordplay, assonance, and alliteration, an initial learning of his craft, a prelude to his transposing of the primitive skills in this poem into his own mature technique and voice. Furthermore, in another poem, "Lines to Myself," we observe the poet goading himself into a more trenchant, forceful style:

> In poetry I wish you would
> Avoid the lilting platitude.
> Give us poems, humped and strong,
> Laced tight with thongs of song.
> Poems that explode in silence

Without forcing, without violence.
Whose music is strong and clear and good
Like a saw zooming in seasoned wood.
You should attempt concrete compression,
Half guessing, half expression.

And here both the advice and the style itself anticipate the course Heaney was to follow.

His rapid maturing as a poet who some four years later would publish an impressive first book is not entirely surprising. During this relatively brief period that I have been discussing, a number of literary stimuli seem to have converged for Heaney into a provisional poetics, a poetics for which he required some form of confirmation, of validation. A poetry of fuselages or of sociology was not authentic for him; what was, a poetry concerned with nature, the shocks and discoveries of childhood experience on a farm, the mythos of the locale—in short, a regional poetry—was essentially a counter-poetry, decidedly not fashionable at the time. To write such poetry called for a measure of confidence if not outright defiance. Indeed, Anthony Thwaite in his *New Statesman* review of *Door into the Dark* sees the authenticity of the poems but finds their appeal exotic, adding wryly, "Turbines and pylons for the 1930s: bulls for the 1960s. It's an odd progression." And a number of reviewers misleadingly have linked the poet with the Georgians, who relatively speaking played over the bucolic surface of nature whereas Heaney digs into the archetypal roots and into the psychic roots of his own being as well. As John Press says in his article, regionalism "may lend itself to a kind of universality which escapes the poetry of men whose material is derived from a study of contemporary politics." Put another way, it is what the poet does with his donné that matters. If the result is effective it makes little difference whether the poet begins with bulls or, as in the case of Alan Ginsberg, with supermarkets or other heterogeneous details of American culture.

Two poets in particular, it seems clear, served to release the young poet's latent purposes, to offer the validation he required. Frost was one, certainly a pivotal figure for Heaney. Benedict Kiely, in his *Hollins Critic* article, "A raid into Dark Corners: the Poetry of Seamus Heaney," reports the poet's saying "that the first poet who ever spoke to him was Robert Frost." "Leaving stains upon the tongue and lust for picking," a line in "Blackberry-Picking" (*Death of a Naturalist*) which bears an imprint of Frost's "After Apple Picking," is only one of a number of resemblances showing how well the Irish poet heard the American: both poets excel at rendering physical detail and sense experience. And Heaney must have noticed in Frost a poet who went against the grain of obvious experimentalism in his era and wrote verse in traditional forms—traditional forms but charged with the rhythms of natural speech. He must have noticed other characteristics too: a vision of nature which includes dark forces as well as benign ones; the human pain and tragedy suffered as profoundly by rural inhabitants as by others; the combining of matter of fact with transcendental inclinations; the appreciation of native skills and disciplines which have their correspondences to the art of poetry. (The poet informs me, incidentally, that although he was generally unenthusiastic about farm work and not especially adept—like Frost—the one exception was his skill with a

pitchfork, for which he earned some local acclaim.)
Heaney, however, did not become a servile imitator even
though specific signs of Frost's influence persist, with
decreasing frequency, into *Wintering Out*, his most recent volume. He had found a twentieth-century model
for the kind of poetry he desired to write, a model more
recent than, say, Wordsworth or Clare, and he set about
creating work that in theme and style diverges markedly
from Frost's.

The other poet is Ted Hughes, whose poetry he came
upon around 1962, and who provided a contemporary
source of encouragement, a reinforcement of that given
by Frost. One can perceive what this English poet
meant, and still means, to Heaney when we read him
saying in his review of Hughes's *Selected Poems* ("Deep
as England" in *Hibernia*, December 1, 1972) that
"Hughes brought back into English poetry an unsentimental intimacy with the hidden country. Probably not
since John Clare had the outback of hedge and farmyard
been viewed so urgently." But that intimacy goes deeper
with both poets than hedge and farmyard; Heaney says
that in Hughes's poetry "racial memory, animal instinct
and poetic inspiration all flow into one another," and he
might as well be speaking of his own poetry, a point
that should become apparent in the course of this study.
With an exception or two—"the last wolf killed in
Britain" in Hughes's "February" and "the wolf has died
out/ In Ireland" in Heaney's "Midnight" (*Wintering
Out*)—it is not a matter of direct parallels or borrow-
ings: superficial comparisons are easy enough to find in
the rank, brute particulars of nature exploited by both
poets. More important are the general affinities as, for

example, the attraction of the archetypal and pagan for both. And Heaney's statement about Hughes, "It is not enough to praise his imagery for 'its admirable violence' or its exact sensuousness," could again refer to himself. He says that the chief effect on him was in the matter of diction, and the similarity here is pronounced: in both poets words erupt with kinesthetic and visceral force; a line will turn on a deliberately "unpoetic" word. Heaney speaks for both when he says, "Into the elegant, iambic and typically standard English intonations of contemporary verse he interjected an energetic, heavily stressed, consciously extravagant and inventive northern voice." Even here, however, it is not a case of direct borrowing; Heaney, as the sudden outpouring of his poems suggested, had his own inner hoard of language. Hughes was a fortuitous example. As John Press says, it was not so much discipleship: Hughes "saved [him] from making a false start." The important thing is that as he was getting started Heaney felt affinities with a number of poets, from Wordsworth to Hughes, who helped reveal to him his own resources.

Superseding literary influences and affinities in importance are the poet's identification with place and his intense engagement with language. These, I believe, would have enabled him to survive any false start. "Our poesy is as a gum which oozes/ From whence tis nourished": he is fond of this utterance by the poet in *Timon of Athens* and has quoted it more than once, one occasion being in an article he wrote for *The Guardian* in May, 1972, "The Trade of an Irish Poet," a key statement on the origins of his poetry. Press quotes him as saying that "Wordsworth was lucky and . . . I was lucky

in having this kind of rich, archetypal subject matter . . . as part of growing up." Whereas Frost vitiated
some of his poetry by becoming too often the poseur of
his region, Heaney writes out of what is inextricably his
birthright. Rural life itself has a rhythm determined by
the cycle of the seasons and the round of tasks; it becomes a ritual of the land. Birth and death, immediate
events, are parts of that rhythm too. In this setting a
child's life has its full quota of drama, real terrors merg-
ing into the realm of legend: "the bog was rushy and
treacherous," Heaney reports in the *Guardian* article,
"no place for children. They said you shouldn't go near
the moss-holes because 'there was no bottom in them.' "

And in this setting the landmarks of Irish history and
myth project themselves into present consciousness.
Benedict Kiely tells us that "Rody McCorley, the patri-
ot boy renowned in balladry, was hanged at the Bridge
of Toome in 1798" and he continues,

> To the west of the loughshore are the Sperrin mountains
> to which O'Neill withdrew between Kinsale and his final
> flight to Europe. Glanconkyne, where he stayed for a while,
> has a complicated mythology associated with the autumn
> festival of Lugh, the father, in the mythologies, of Cuchul-
> lain. The mountains are plentifully marked by pre-Celtic
> standing stones and stone circles.

Thus it is an area where history, with its battles, heroes,
subjections, and famines, flows back into prehistory,
legend, and myth. In this rich primal material not only
does the past inform the present but fable and land are
conjoined, and it is against this background that one
takes on a clear but complicated identity.

Looking back now, Heaney can see that he grew up in
a center that did hold. Despite the history of discord

and the recent eruption of conflict and violence that has so horribly blighted life in Northern Ireland, he did as a boy experience comparative stability. Catholics, the majority in his area, lived in relative harmony with the Protestants, a sharp awareness of differences notwithstanding. (George Evans, a Protestant neighbor, on one occasion brought rosary beads back from Rome and presented them to the Heaneys: "I stole them from the Pope's dresser," he said.) The differences were inescapable, however. Heaney says, again in the *Guardian* article, that in Mossbawn, between Castledawson and Toome, he was "symbolically placed between the marks of English influence and the lure of the native experience, between 'the demesne' [Moyola Park, now occupied by Lord Moyola, formerly Major James Chicester-Clark, ex-Unionist Prime Minister] and the 'bog'. . . The demesne was walled, wooded, beyond our ken."

This symbolic split has meant that the poet writes out of a dual perspective, and it has had special import for the language of his poetry. "The seeds," he has told me, "were in language, words." Even when a youth, before he was struck by any overt urge to write poems, individual words were compelling, to be mulled over in the mind. With more self-awareness now he can analyze the twin sources of his language, the literary words and the words of place, of origins or, put another way, the English and the native. Is Mossbawn, he wonders in the *Guardian* essay, a Scots-English word meaning the planter's house on the bog, or since "we pronounced it Moss Bann, and ban is the Gaelic word for white," might it not mean "the white moss, the moss of bog cotton? In the syllables of my home I see a metaphor of the split

culture of Ulster." The names of the nearby townlands
of Broagh and Anahorish "are forgotten Gaelic music in
the throat, *bruach* and *anach fhior uisce*, the riverbank
and the place of clear water," and they made their way
into two of the poems in *Wintering Out* for which they
serve as subject and title. Two other names in the immediate area, Grove Hill and Back Park, "insist that this
familiar locale is a version of pastoral"; "Grove is a word
that I associate with translations of the classics." His
auditory imagination prefers another name, "The Dir-
raghs, from *doire* as in Derry," but nonetheless Spenser
and Sir John Davies, who played their parts in the crush-
ing of the indigenous culture, are also as poets figures
who command his attention, contributing to the complex education one receives in this "split culture." The
article concludes with this paragraph:

> Certainly the secret of being a poet, Irish or otherwise, lies
> in the summoning and meshing of the subconscious and
> semantic energies of words. But my quest for precision and
> definition, while it may lead backward, is conducted in the
> living speech of a landscape that I was born with. If you
> like, I began as a poet when my roots were crossed with my
> reading. I think of the personal and Irish pieties as vowels,
> and the literary awareness nourished on English as conso-
> nants. My hope is that the poems will be vocables adequate
> to my whole experience.

Although he wants his idiom to adhere closely to the
speech he was born with this does not mean that the
effort should be methodical and deliberate, an effort to
apply rigidly the view, "formulated most coherently by
Thomas McDonagh," the scholar-activist slain in the
1916 uprising, that "the distinctive note of Irish poetry
is struck when the rhythms and assonances of Gaelic
poetry insinuate themselves into the texture of English

verse." Sympathetic to the attempts of Austin Clarke and others to apply Gaelic techniques systematically, he finds "the whole enterprise a bit programmatic." It is better, he implies, to trust to one's roots and let the language of the poems arise naturally. This is what he has done, to singular advantage.

He is conscious of other divisions as well. Press quotes him as having experienced an "exile from a way of life which I was brought up to . . . from a farming community to an academic . . . exile in time . . . from childhood." This exile has resulted in an acute search into his cultural roots, accentuated by his moving in the conflicting worlds of Mossbawn-Belfast, Ulster-Ireland-England, Ireland-America. The search has been inward too, into the sources of self, which are also, ultimately, the sources of poetry. Further, he is a Catholic poet and fully aware of inner tensions the Catholic is heir to; constantly redeemed and constantly instilled with guilt. Benedict Kiely reports his saying, "Penance indeed was a sacrament that rinsed and renewed . . . but although it did give a momentary release from guilt, it kept this sense of sin as inseparable from one's life as one's shadows." But if some of his poems can be said to depend on a Catholic imagination, he has not been content to rest there; he has probed into the unconscious. As he asserts in *The Listener* (February 5, 1970), "circumstances have changed and writing is usually born today out of the dark active centre of the imagination . . . I think this notion of the dark centre, the blurred and irrational storehouse of insight and instincts, the hidden core of the self—this notion is the foundation of what viewpoint I might articulate for myself as a poet."

2

Death of a Naturalist

A number of poems in Heaney's first collection, *Death of a Naturalist*, comment in some way about art and poetry themselves. "Synge on Aran," for example, concludes, "There

he comes now, a hard pen
scraping in his head;
the nib filed on a salt wind
and dipped in the keening sea.

"In Small Townlands," inscribed "For Colin Middleton," a Northern Irish painter, begins with this stanza:

In small townlands his hogshair wedge
Will split the granite from the clay
Till crystal in the rock is bared:
Loaded brushes hone an edge
On mountain blue and heather grey.
Outcrops of stone contract, outstared.

In "Digging," the opening poem in the volume and a declaration of the poet's purpose and function, the speaker, armed with his "squat pen" resting "snug as a gun" "Between my finger and my thumb," observes his father below the window digging "among the flowerbeds" and reflects on the way his father twenty years before rhythmically dug "through potato drills," and then on his grandfather's turf-cutting prowess. Thinking of their precise, efficient mastery, he asserts at the end of the poem, "But I've no spade to follow men like them." The pen is his tool: "I'll dig with it."

The artistic tools required for the aesthetic that declares itself in these examples are hard, sharp, penetrating; they scrape, split, hone, and dig, fine instruments for revealing underlying shapes—for sculpting. "In Small Townlands" most clearly suggests sculpting, suggests in fact something of the early lapidary method of H. D. (Hilda Doolittle). I do not mean to imply a direct or conscious derivation from the Imagists, however. These qualities simply pervade twentieth-century poetry and Heaney would easily have assimilated them in his reading; it is not a matter of imitation. Sculptural incisiveness is just one of the characteristics of style in *Death of a Naturalist.*

What chiefly makes these early pcems Heaney's own is another, complementary quality. Put briefly, it is a sensuous, vital energy which determines their diction, imagery, and prosody. To an unusual degree details register with an immediacy on the reader's senses. Note for example this image in "Death of a Naturalist": "the warm thick slobber/ of frogspawn that grew like clotted water." Much of the effect derives from the gross, labial "slobber," but in "clotted water" the substance verbally thickens into tangible density. Similarly, the cream of "Churning Day" becomes "coagulated sunlight" as the curd turns into butter; first it was "A thick crust, coarse-grained as limestone rought-cast," which "hardened gradually on top of the four crocks," with the limestone simile and the appropriate hard c's vividly realizing the solid *appearance* of the crusted cream, yet one would be surprised to discover that his hand could break through that surface. Similarly the decisive and accurate proficiency of the grandfather "Nicking and slicing neatly" into the turf is realized in the technique of the poem, the immaculate arrangement of sounds in the phrase rendering kinetically the skillfull physical action (the hard c of "Nicking" changed into the smooth c of "slicing," the necessarily fastidious pronunciation of the syllables emphasized by the alliteration of the n's). This same conjunction of precision and sensuousness is evident in these lines in "At a Potato Digging":

> The cold smell of potato mould, the squelch and slap
> Of soggy peat, the curt cuts of an edge
> Through living roots awaken in my head.

The unexpected but right words "squelch and slap" for the sogginess and "curt cuts" for the sharp edge, the repetitions of sound, the olfactory, aural, tactile, and visual impressions—"in my head," yes, but almost visceral: these make it difficult to draw a clear line separating poetic artifice and physical reality, which is as it should be, the two becoming one in the body of the poem.

It is also through such physical immediacy of word and image that Heaney creates emotional impact:

> A scythe's edge, a clean spade, a pitch-fork's prongs:
> Slowly bright objects formed when you went in.
> Then you felt cobwebs clogging up your lungs . . .

These lines in "The Barn," with their series of potentially lethal sharp objects and the claustrophobic cobweb image, cause us to experience the ominousness within the barn and prepare us for the nightmarish effect in the final two stanzas of the poem, where the speaker recalls the intrusion into his dreams of the terrors harbored in the dark barn, the images of day converted into sources of fear. The import of "The Early Purges" depends much on the reader's feeling a pathos in the deliberate, heartlessly matter-of-fact drowning of kittens, and this pathos is produced in the poem by the physically convincing disposal of the creatures, which make "a frail metal sound" when pitched into a bucket of water, "Soft paws scraping like mad. But their tiny din/ Was soon soused"; "Like wet gloves they bobbed and shone." "Frail metal sound" and "tiny din," are precisely evocative of the kittens' panic. One is not to indulge, however, in the "false sentiments" of the sadness and fear the speaker felt as a six-year-old as he witnessed the drowning of the "scraggy wee shits" by Dan Taggart; "The Early Purges" ends on a note of cruel wisdom— " 'Prevention of cruelty' talk cuts ice in town/ Where they consider death unnatural,/ But on well-run farms pests have to be kept down"—and so at the end the reader is caught in the tension between the acutely felt pathos and a relentless logic reminiscent of Frost's lessons. I have dwelt on such examples, and they could be multiplied, because they show distinguishing traits of Heaney's early style; they indicate, I believe, what Christopher Ricks and C. B. Cox had in mind when in their favorable reviews in the *New Statesman* and *Spectator* they spoke, respectively, of the "unsentimental clarity which impinges with a sense of the physical" and the "sensual pleasure in verbs of action, in onomatopoeic recreations of physical movement."

Augmenting the physical authenticity and the clean, decisive art of the best of the early poems, mainly the ones concerned with the impact of the recollected initiatory experiences of childhood and youth, is the human voice that speaks in them. At its most distinctive it is unpretentious, open, modest, and yet poised, aware, fundamentally serious despite its occasional humorous or ironic turn. Within an anecdotal, sometimes colloquial, or matter-of-fact context it can be terse, suddenly dramatic, charged with emotion, shock or wonder breaking through understatement. It is flexible, open to modulations and complexities of tone. Generally the rhythms are natural though in accord with the predominant pattern and metrics of a given poem. The form is quite free in "Dawn Shoot," which for the most part hovers between blank and free verse, and the rhythms approach those of taut prose:

> Donelly's left hand came up
> And came down on my barrel. This one was his.
> "For Christ's sake," I spat, "Take your time, there'll be
>   more."
> There was the playboy trotting up to the hole
> By the ash tree, "Wild rover no more,"
> Said Donnelly and emptied two barrels
> And got him. I finished him off.

By contrast, in "At a Potato Digging" the form is more strict, as in this opening quatrain:

> A mechanical digger wrecks the drill,
> Spins up a dark shower of roots and mould.
> Labourers swarm in behind, stoop to fill
> Wicker creels. Fingers go dead in the cold.

Even in this poem, in which the pulse is more deliberate, in keeping with both the angry elegy for those who were caught in the great famine and the celebration of the laborers' perserverence and the ritual nature of their work—the poem ends with libations and a sense of propitiation—the metrical variations accord with the directness of the account. Now, this is not an exceptional example; it lacks, except superficially in the details of potato farming, the poet's indelible stamp. Nor would I begin to claim for it the mastery of Yeats or Frost, but it does show that he had learned something of their skill in crossing natural speech with traditional verse structure: form and a living speech working together.

In "Death of a Naturalist," which he later astutely chose as the title poem for his first book, Heaney most successfully exploited the qualities I have described so far. The poem begins with seemingly matter-of-fact description:

> All year the flax-dam festered in the heart
> Of the townland; green and heavy headed
> Flax had rotted there, weighted down by huge sods.
> Daily it sweltered in the punishing sun.
> Bubbles gargled delicately, bluebottles
> Wove a strong gauze of sound around the smell.
> But best of all was the warm thick slobber
> Of frogspawn that grew like clotted water
> In the shade of the banks.

This makes palpable the details of the hot, rank, peaceful scene which fascinated the young boy, wakening his innocent curiosity and pleasure. But the description prepares for the grotesque initiation he would undergo on a later occasion: in the full context of the poem the phrase "festered in the heart" implies a human sickness at the core; the "strong gauze of sound" is a deceptive screen "around the smell"; "festered," "gauze," and "smell" form a subliminal image of infected wounds.

His teacher set up another screen around the reality of nature, domesticating, "humanizing" the gross sexuality of the frogs: "Miss Walls would tell us how/ The daddy frog was called a bullfrog/ And how he croaked and how the mammy frog/ Laid hundreds of little eggs and this was/ Frogspawn." And how comforting was the fact that you could tell the weather by the frogs, "yellow in the sun and brown/ In rain," as though nature operated for man's benefit and the sun were not "punishing." This feeble, polite and sentimental gloss on nature, however, was rudely upset for the boy one day when the "angry frogs/ Invaded the flax-dam" and produced "a coarse croaking that I had not heard/ Before."

> The air was thick with a bass chorus.
> Right down the dam gross-bellied frogs were cocked
> On sods; their loose necks pulsed like sails. Some hopped:
> The slap and plop were obscene threats. Some sat
> Poised like mud grenades, their blunt heads farting.
> I sickened, turned, and ran. The great slime kings
> Were gathered there for vengeance and I knew
> That if I dipped my hand the spawn would clutch it.

Like ugly fearsome father-figures in a depraved fairy tale, the "great slime kings," gathered it would seem for some malignant ritual, suggest primeval forces, all in nature that is alien, outside man's control. At the same time, however, they represent the animality in man, the whole nexus of the sexual and cloacal burden. Disturbingly phallic, they were "cocked" and "their loose necks pulsed like sails." "The slap and plop," "like mud grenades," "their blunt heads farting": no wonder the boy felt an obscene threat and feared being seized by the unnameable force (so particularized in the oozy spawn) which he sensed unconsciously must be a part of his fate as an adult. The poem is uniquely Heaney's, the high point of his achievement at this stage of his development. The details at the end are at once true to the nauseating reality of the frogs and to their surreal psychological implications—all the obscure but immediate sexual turmoil of puberty and adolescence nightmarishly concentrated, erupting in the repulsive images.

To consider the volume as a whole, however, is to become aware of its unevenness; we should not expect every poem to reach the level of "Death of a Naturalist." As the poet tested his new-found skills with a variety of subjects and modes, he wrote some poems in which technique turns into manner. Now and then, for example, the attempt to infuse the poems with energy degenerates into forced metaphor. "Waterfall" begins splendidly:

The burn drowns steadily in its own downpour,
A helter-skelter of muslin and glass
That skids to a halt, crashing up suds.

The almost hidden analogy of a car which "skids to a halt, crashing" is just enough to intensify the impression of motion and shattering impact, but then it becomes obvious and intrusive: "Simultaneous acceleration/ And sudden braking"; "It appears an athletic glacier has reared into reverse." "Trout" also begins strongly, with ellipsis and a dramatic image of the latent power in the fish: "Hangs, a fat gun-barrel,/ Deep under arched bridges"; the motionlessness is highly charged. The main device after this is an extension of the gun image— "muzzle," "bull's eye," "picks off," "torpedoed," "fired," "reported," "darts like a tracer-/ bullet," "volley," and "ramrodding." The marvel of the trout's speed and power, yes, but the result is poetically static, the impact of the poem is reduced by the excess of imagistic ingenuity. Ordinance and military terms in this poem and others threaten to become a metaphorical tic. Still, the central metaphor of military action in "Dawn Shoot"—"challenged," "sentry," "reconnaissance," "all clear," and so on—works very well, for it characterizes the excitement and bravado of the two boys in the poem as they insensitively violate nature by their amoral, ruthless shooting of their prey; it also supplies a subtle irony: war games.

Not unexpectedly, as in "Digging" and "Mid-Term Break," Heaney was drawn to his own family for some of his subject matter and the results are mixed. "Follower" runs the risk of being a standard father-son poem. (In fact, Giles Sadler in *The Review*, October, 1966, complains, "We have heard this before, in MacBeth's father's mining helmet, or in Connor's grand-dad toiling at the forge." Sadler is piqued because Faber and Faber published the book, therby urging "reputation on virtuosity.") But it rises above this limitation. The speaker recalls his hero-worship of his father, "An expert," almost a demi-god, "His shoulders globed like a full sail strung/ Between the shafts and the furrow"; "I stumbled in his hob-nailed wake" (a line written before Heaney discovered Roethke but an indication of how receptive he would be to that poet's work). But what saves the poems is the ending:

> I was a nuisance, tripping, falling,
> Yapping always. But today
> It is my father who keeps stumbling
> Behind me, and will not go away.

In its sudden reversal it pulls tight the ring of life's inevitable sequence, turning hero-worship and possible nostalgia for the past into present pain and resentment over his now-failing father. "Ancestral Photograph," however, is a polished nostalgic set-piece which expresses regret for the passing of the local cattle fairs. Using the standard device of the family photograph as a basis for its lament, such a poem might have been written by any number of Irish poets. The speaker watched his father sadden "when the fairs stopped," and the poem ends with neat finality: "Closing this chapter of our chronicle/ I take your uncle's portrait to the attic."

And family history leads to Irish history. How can an Irish poet avoid that anguishing and obviously poetic material? The problem is to avoid derivation, rehearsing a subject in a slightly different way when such poems have become standard in the repertoire of Ireland's poets. "At a Potato Digging," to which I have already referred, is the longest poem in the volume and skillfully sustains its homage to the present workers and their forebears who succumbed to famine. Here is a poem in a lineage with Kavanagh's "The Great Hunger" but basically in Heaney's own idiom: "these knobbed and slit-eyed tubers seem/ the petrified hearts of drills. Split/ by the spade, they show white as cream." Its pathos and bitter recall are controlled by grim concision and clipped rhythm: "Mouths tightened in, eyes died hard,/ faces chilled to a plucked bird." The only question I would raise concerns the predictable effect of the pattern of religious imagery—"Processional," "humbled knees," "a seasonal altar of the sod," "breaking timeless fasts," "faithless," "Libations"—even in a poem concerning "fear and homage to the famine god." "For the Commander of the 'Eliza'," with a quotation from Cecil Woodham-Smith's *The Great Hunger* as epigraph, is spoken by an English naval officer sensitive to a group of desperate, starving natives, whom he hailed in Gaelic though he refused to help them. The poem's bitterness and sorrow are filtered through his mingled sympathy, self-concern ("Less incidents the better") and dutiful matter-of-factness. Terse irony controls the sense of outrage and pain:

> Sir James, I understand, urged free relief
> For famine victims in the Westport sector
> And earned tart reprimand from good Whitehall.
> Let natives prosper by their own exertions;
> Who could not swim might go ahead and sink.
> 'The Coast Guard with their zeal and activity
> Are too lavish' were the words, I think.

It is a moving poem but the irony is almost too deft.

In a few satirical poems Heaney focuses on the contemporary scene. The strongest and sharpest is "Docker," a biting depiction of a Protestant bigot; his obtuseness, inarticulate rage, and warped Calvinism are etched, perhaps too insistently, in the imagery of his only real religion—work: "God is a foreman with certain definite views," "sledgehead jaw," "the lips' vice," "Mosaic imperatives bang home like rivets," "A factory horn will blare the Resurrection." The moral vacuum of intolerance and hate turns in upon himself and his family: "Tonight the wife and children will be quiet/ At slammed door and smoker's cough in the hall." This understated satire is artful in the manner of the Fifties, but following the line, "That fist would drop a hammer on a Catholic," the speaker's seemingly flat interjection, "Oh yes, that kind of thing could start again," is loaded with a hard knowledge that cuts through any qualifications about style. On first glance "Poor Women in a City Church," which follows "Docker," appears no more than a sympathetic, indeed sentimental, response to the women's devotion, but a closer reading precludes this impression. With Browningesque irony the speaker conveys the oppressiveness of the scene: "Cold yellow candle-tongues, blue flame/ Mince and caper as whispered calls/ Take wing up to the Holy Name." As the "Old dough-faced women with black shawls/ Drawn down tight kneel in the stalls" they are consoled by the atmosphere and decor of religion, not by its spiritual depth; the "Golden shrines, altar lace,/ Marble columns and cool shadows" are what "Still them." They seem as lifeless as the candles: "In the gloom you cannot trace/ A wrinkle on their beeswax brows." If the satire is more muted, these Catholic women are nonetheless counterparts of the docker.

The love poems in *Death of a Naturalist* are unpretentious and direct in their feelings yet undistinguished. More complex poems on this subject were to appear in the two volumes to follow. In several instances the conception is too neatly clinched: for example, "You've gone, I am at sea./ Until you resume command/ Self is mutiny" ("Valediction"). "Twice Shy," about two lovers tremulously holding back their excitement "As hawk and prey apart," nicely balances its seriousness by a lightness of tone and detail: "Her scarf *à la* Bardot"; "Our juvenilia/ Had taught us both to wait,/ Not to publish feeling"; "Mushroom loves already/ Had puffed

and burst in hate." But the Bardot reference is appropriate for a poem which adds little new to the methods of
the previous decade.

None of the poems just discussed is embarrassingly
poor; in fact they would suffice very well as stock for
any young poet setting up in trade. But about a third of
the poems in this first book—"Death of a Naturalist,"
"Dawn Shoot," "The Early Purges," "The Barn," "Digging," "An Advancement of Learning," "Churning Day,"
"Blackberry-Picking" plus a few more—established
Heaney's as a voice to be reckoned with. The successes
arose from his risktaking, the virtuoso prosody, the bold
word choices, the delving into the potentially sentimental subject matter of recollected childhood and adolescent experience on a farm. Dangers lay in the method.
The words, for instance, that so characterize his style,
Heaney words such as slobber, soused, plumped,
knobbed, and clotted, are susceptible to overuse, to the
possibility of eventual self-parody, though it was by running this danger that he gained an earthy concreteness;
also his diction would undergo a continuing evolution in
the succeeding two volumes. He would extend and
deepen his subject matter, too, and one means of advance would be to explore more fully those forces
underlying plain sense and observation. While the hazel
rod lies dead in the hands of others, the subject of "The
Diviner" is attuned to an irrational power. The final
poem in this book, "Personal Helicon," is as Michael
Longley says in his essay on Ulster poetry in *Causeway: the Arts in Ulster* "both credo and manifesto"; its
concluding sentence, "I rhyme/ To see myself, to set the
darkness echoing," brings us to the threshold of the
second book of poems.

3

Door into the Dark

"All I know is a door into the dark," the first line of "The Forge," draws the reader, as does the book's title itself, into the thematic heart of the second collection, the center around which most of its poems cohere, thus making *Door into the Dark* more unified than *Death of a Naturalist*. Heaney is quoted in *The Listener* (February 5, 1970) as saying, "Good writing, like good smitty [sic] work, is a compound of energy and artifice," and the inner darkness in "The Forge" is the setting for a labor and a skill based on an integrity to "beat real iron out." But the blacksmith is more than a craftsman; he comes to symbolize the shaper, a kind of "leather-aproned" Hephaestus, "hairs in his nose," who creates in a mythological and ritualistic dimension:

The anvil must be somewhere in the centre,
Horned as a unicorn, at one end square,
Set there immoveable: an altar
Where he expends himself in shape and music.

In this sonnet the blacksmith performs magically, religiously, in harmony with the dark powers. The artisan in "Thatcher" performs his wonders in the light of day, stitching "all together/ Into a sloped honeycomb" which leaves beholders "gaping at his Midas touch." He and the blacksmith taken together preside over the worlds of light and dark; their traditional skills are practical, of the earth, yet occult too. Much further back in time the monks "In Gallarus Oratory"—"A core of old dark walled up with stone/ A yard thick" out at the end of Dingle Peninsula—found both themselves and a true holiness by submitting to the dark. Immersion in the primordial prepared them for their King and for a mystical vision of earth, "The sea a censer, and grass a flame." To go inside the unmortared walls of the oratory is to plunge to the chthonic center, or as it is put in the poem: "When you're in it alone/ You might have dropped, a reduced creature/ To the heart of the globe." Earth and the spiritual are not divorced; light and dark are parts of a total vision.

The aesthetic implications of this knowledge are, of the poems in *Door into the Dark*, most clear in "The Peninsula," which insists on the necessity for constant renewal of vision by submitting to the dark. "When you have nothing more to say, just drive/ For a day all round the peninsula." At night when "you're in the dark again" recall the details observed during the day, and then

> drive back home, still with nothing to say
> Except that now you will uncode all landscapes
> By this: things founded clean on their own shapes,
> Water and ground in their extremity.

In the dark—of the imagination it would seem—the things of day are revealed in their full luminousness: "the glazed foreshore and silhouetted log" or

"Islands riding themselves out into the fog." Such preternatural clarity prepares one to see all landscapes, just as the monks were prepared for the vision of day.

Other poems, however, concern those atavistic, mysterious, disturbing and vital forces that lie submerged in nature and in our being, dark, irrational forces not so amenable to the imagination, though it is necessary for the imagination to deal with them, as Heaney does in "The Outlaw." The outlaw in this poem is an unlicensed bull used for the illegal servicing of a "nervous Friesian" cow, performing his duty with "the unfussy ease of a good tradesman," "Unhurried as an old steam engine shunting," "impassive as a tank,/ Dropping off like a tipped-up load of sand"—the images of mechanical power paradoxically conveying the instinctive power he holds in reserve. "He slammed life home" before he, "in his own time, resumed the dark, the straw." The speaker could not guess why he "gave Old Kelly the clammy silver," risking a fine, but it made him an outlaw too, an initiate at the brute rite, and the Friesian was mated with that untamed, dark power symbolized in the bull. In style, situation, and theme "The Outlaw" is a point of liaison between key poems in *Death of a Naturalist* and *Door into the Dark*.

But the opening poem in the second book, "Night-Piece," adds radically to Heaney's stylistic resources as it probes the dark center from another direction:

Must you know it again?
Dull pounding through hay,
The uneasy whinny.

A sponge lip drawn off each separate tooth.

Opalescent haunch,
Muscle and hoof

Bundled under the roof.

Terse, remarkably compressed, disquieting, and more
oblique than is the poet's wont, the poem, particularly
in the telling details of the second stanza, evokes a
nightmarish animality, some undefined dread, that has
been obsessively relived again and again in all its vividness, at a point where dream and reality intersect.
Another possible suggestion arises: Is the title a sardon-
ic sexual play on words and the horse imagery—"dull
pounding through hay" and so on—a means of charac-
terizing human sexuality when reduced to grotesque animality by the absence of all but the physical? If so, the
poem becomes more disturbing, but either way it opens
the book on an uneasy, intriguing note. "Gone," which
follows and is less radical in style, expresses poignant
regret for the loss of the animality "Night-Piece" concerns. Gone is the pungent reality of the life force repre-
sented by a horse which broke free from its stable "Clad
only in shods"; "His hot reek is lost./ The place is old in
his must." The lifelessness remaining is finely captured
in the description of the man-made equipment he left
behind: "Green froth that lathered each end/ Of the
shining bit/ Is a cobweb of grass-dust"; "Reins, chains
and traces/ Droop in a tangle." In "Dream," the third
poem, the speaker, in the graphically immediate reality
of nightmare, was with a billhook "hacking a stalk/
Thick as a telegraph pole" (what could be more phallic?) Then

The next stroke
Found a man's head under the hook.

Before I woke
I heard the steel stop
In the bone of the brow.

No strict Freudian interpretation is needed; the object of the violence does not have to be the speaker's father. It is quite enough that the wielder of the hook has imbedded it in the unconscious, in the primal source of sexual guilt and destructiveness. All the murderousness of Cain is in him. The door opens into this aspect of the darkness too. These three opening poems, especially "Night-Piece" and "Dream," create an unsettling impact and preclude a simple response to the poems in the book as a whole, which vary in tone and implication though focused on the often inexplicable dark powers.

One retains a keen awareness that these elemental, timeless powers are potentially uncontrollable, but rooted in the same ultimate source are more benign energies, mysterious influences deep in things, which it is man's business to recognize if not fully comprehend. Thus there runs through many of the poems in the volume a celebration of earthly things, of the life force, along with an attempt to chart those influences, those gravities that pull us toward the center, and a desire to plumb depths even if, as the final words in the volume have it, the "centre is bottomless." "Whinlands" illustrates very clearly the tough force of survival in the whin. In a fire, only its thorns burn; "This stunted, dry richness/ Persists on hills, near stone ditches,/ Over flint-bed and battlefield." Even an old guitar ("Victorian Guitar") can become the symbol of latent life. The husband of the young woman who, according to its inscription, owned it before her marriage "cannot have known [the bride's] touch," cannot have known tenderness, love, music, sexual fulfillment, or life. Now the man who owns the guitar is giving it "the time of its life." In "Rite of Spring" ropes of straw are burned around a frozen pump to free it. The effect of the poem depends chiefly on the double-entendre of the last two lines: "It cooled, we lifted her latch,/ Her entrance was wet, and she came." Whether or not we accept the stroke of wit here, and I believe it is saved by the earthy farm context and the colloquial personification—the sudden shift is both surprising and right for the sense of primal release—it is certainly not the "prim-lipped sexual metaphor" that A. Alvarez (another critic upset because Faber and Faber inflates the reputations of young poets by publishing them) calls it in his derogatory review in the *Observer*.

To celebrate the life force is to celebrate fertility and both lead, in *Door into the Dark*, to the area of myth and archetype. In "Requiem for the Croppies," a sonnet based on historical event and more ambitious than the poems just discussed, those free-spirited fellows played havoc with the opposing organized military forces until they themselves were slaughtered "on Vinegar Hill, the fatal conclave." But although they were unceremoniously buried where they fell the barley which they had carried in their pockets for sustenance "grew up out of the grave," nourished by their blood. Here historical fact merges into mythical overtones: these heroes died like fertility gods in the spring, the continuity of nature preserved. The events are recounted with vivid succinctness by one of the dead croppies, yet in keeping with a requiem, the tone is stately, mingling grief and nobility.

On a less formal level, "Undine" gracefully celebrates the procreative force by weaving together the essentials of the myth and a farmer's act of clearing his ditches so water can flow along them. This mundane work is described by Undine in sexual metaphors that arise naturally from the situation: the feelings are both sensual and reverent, reminding the reader that Undine gains a soul by marrying a mortal and bearing a child: "he dug a spade deep in my flank/ And took me to him"; "I alone/ Could give him subtle increase and reflection"; "Each limb/ Lost its cold freedom. Human, warmed to him." Compared with this poem "Girls Bathing, Galway 1965" is more rhetorical—"The breakers pour/ Themselves into themselves, the years/ Shuttle through space invisibly" and "generations sighing in/ The salt suds where the wave has crashed/ Labour in fear of flesh and sin"—but it explicitly points to one of the poet's strengths, the transcending of matter-of-factness within a seemingly commonplace setting. The poem asserts that "No milk-limbed Venus ever rose/ Miraculous on this western shore"; and "our sterner myth" of "A pirate queen in battle clothes" seems to have dissolved with time. What predominates at the end, belying "fear of flesh and sin," is the fresh beauty, innocence, and joy of the girls: "Bare-legged, smooth-shouldered and long-backed/ They wade ashore with skips and shouts," if not in classical nude glory then in "swimsuits" but not in the battle garb of the native pirate queen. "So Venus comes, matter-of-fact."

An increasing maturity of style in this book of poems is paralleled by deepening insight, particularly noticeable in two love poems and two from women's points of view and spoken by them. The speaker in "Night Drive" recounts his driving south across France toward the woman he addresses, when his senses were heightened by "The smells of ordinariness." The places passed took on something of an epochal importance though unexceptional in themselves: "Montreuil, Abbéville, Beauvais/ . . ./ Each place granting its name's fulfillment." The expression of love, close to sentimentality, finds its correlative in an expansive geographical metaphor: "I thought of you continuously/ A thousand miles south where Italy/ Laid its loin to France on the darkened sphere." This figure, with the speaker feeling that earth itself partook of his sexual longing, prepares for the final declaration, "Your ordinariness was renewed there." Again a sense of the exalted informs the ordinary, yet this is subtly placed against hints of life and extinction, a pattern of mortality which validates the feeling of love and cancels a possible sentimental effect: "A combine . . ./ Bled seeds across its work-light./ A forest fire smouldered out./ One by one small cafés shut," and finally, "the darkened sphere," already quoted.

The suggestions of mortality are more pronounced in "At Ardboe Point," which immediately follows "Night Drive." Here human love is enveloped by "A smoke of flies," actually mosquitoes, which function as both a naturalistic physical presence and a symbolic "invisible veil." They are on the one hand a manifestation of random biological process, insidious in their growth and pervasiveness ("the walls will carry a rash/ Of them, a green pollen") and potentially horrifying seen under magnification: "You'd be looking at a pumping body/

With such outsize beaters for wings" that this would be a visitation "More drastic than Pharaoh's"—here are wit, a touch of humor, and a Donne-like metaphysical shudder. On the other hand the mosquitoes are "our innocent, shuttling/ Choirs, dying through their own empyrean," "troublesome only/ As the last veil on a dancer," the second image carrying an appropriate sexual connotation. Thus the lovers' act when they put out the light and kiss between the sheets will be performed in the ambience of mosquito-ridden mortality and share in the mystery of being; and the darkenss will be a part of their lovemaking and their love.

Fertility and procreation can be agonizing as well as fulfilling, and the pregnant woman in "Mother" pays for her life-giving role with a stifling and gnawing sense of emptiness despite the wild new life in her as she tends to her unrelieved, frustrating chores. She pumps water for the insatiable cows, and the pump and water become an emblem of her own condition. Wind frays "The rope of water I'm pumping./ It pays itself out like air's afterbirth/ At each gulp of the plunger." The bedhead which her husband set in the fence as a gate for the cows is "on its last legs. It does not," she says with a wry sadness, "jingle for joy anymore." Trapped by her sex and the round of necessity, she cries out at the end,

O when I am a gate for myself
Let such wind fray my waters
As scarfs my skirt through my thighs,
Stuffs air down my throat.

The preceding poem, a companion piece really, "The Wife's Tale," emulates those poems of Frost's which dramatize the division between a man and wife. In this

case the husband's world is characterized by power, effi-
ciency, and arrogance. She observes pitchforks "stuck at
angles in the ground/ As javelins might mark lost battle-
fields"; in the quiet of noontime she hears the men's
boots "crunching the stubble twenty yards away"; and
her husband says, "There's good yield,/ Isn't there?—as
proud as if he were the land itself." She, however, has a
sensuous contact with nature unlike his busiensslike approach; "I ran my hand" in the bags of seed; "It was
hard as shot,/ innumerable and cool." He no more
understands her civilizing ritual of spreading a linen
cloth on which to serve the men's meal (playfully mock-
ing her) than she understands just what he expects her
to grasp about his world—"Always this inspection has to
be made/ Even when I don't know what to look for."
Like the land, she must serve as an extension of his ego.
Even so, the husband is not portrayed as a brute, and
though a painful gulf exists between the two (painful
for her at least) their roles complement one another,
and the poem ends on a note of rough pastoral ease, the
men "Spread out, unbuttoned, grateful, under the
trees." Such implications, along with the wife's sensitiv-
ity and her dignified resignation, come through the
seemingly anecdotal recital of her tale. Frost is in the
background, but Heaney has converted the model to his
own uses.

"A Lough Neagh Sequence," a unified suite of seven
poems various in form (mostly quatrains and three-line
stanzas) and taken together the longest poem in *Door
into the Dark*, is the show-piece of the collection, con-
centrating its central themes. It is partly a straightfor-
ward tribute to the stoical eel fishermen (to whom it is

inscribed), who retain the old methods and a sense of fair play, not even learning to swim: "'We'll be quicker going down', they say." The lake itself is marvelous in the root sense of that word, and legendary. "It has virtue that hardens wood to stone./ There is a town sunk beneath its water./ It is a scar left by the Isle of Man." Although the fishermen approach their work pragmatically there is a holiness to it even if they are "Not sensible of any *kyrie*," and although they accept their destiny with understated courage, the rhythm of their labors is part of a larger rhythm they do not consciously comprehend. Like the eels themselves they follow timeless instinctual urges; the wakes of the boats

> are enwound as the catch
> On the morning water: which
> Boat was which?
>
> And when did this begin?
> This morning, last year, when the lough first spawned?
> The crews will answer, "Once the season's in."

The eels embody the central meanings in the sequence, following as they do some mysterious purpose in the endless cycle of procreation and death. The male is as "true/ to his orbit" as the moon's "insinuating pull/ in the ocean." He probes the mud at the dark bottom of the lake, and the female, with uncanny homing instinct makes her way across and through "new trenches, sunk pipes,/ swamps, running streams, the lough" back to the source, thus completing the cycle. Her progress is magical; she goes "silent, wakeless,/ a wisp, a wick that is/ its own taper and light/ through the weltering dark." But to complete the cycle is to recommence it—"Where she's

lost once she lays/ ten thousand feet down in/ her origins." Images of circles, spheres, and coils recur in the
poems, as in the case of the bait (the worms), "Innocent
ventilators of the ground/ Making the globe a perfect
fit."

Part of the total reality symbolized by the eels, however, is the disturbing, irrational aspect of nature. "Vision," the final poem, describes in the third person the
experience of a boy coming upon an eel in the riverbank
fields; "Thick as a birch trunk/ That cable flexed in the
grass/ Every time the wind passed." Years later he
would observe eels moving "through the grass like
hatched fears." To watch them

> Re-wound his world's live girdle.
> Phosphorescent, sinewed slime
> Continued at his feet. Time
> Confirmed the horrid cable.

The whole sequence, then, encompasses this horror, the
dread of mortality, sexuality, and the nonhuman, as
well as the miraculousness of being. The sequence becomes a ritual of life, including the mundane, time and
the timeless, the known and that which transcends
knowledge, the terribly physical and the numinous, the
light and the dark. It is a fine achievement, with the
poet applying his technique to an ambitious aim. What
is best perhaps is the graphic impression we gain of the
eels in all their manifestations, from their wondrousness
to their slimy muscular physicality, the latter enhancing
their symbolic value; as the eels are thrown in a barrel
they become "a knot of back and pewter belly/ That
stays continuously one/ For each catch they fling in/ Is
sucked home like lubrication."

Not every poem in *Door into the Dark* represents an

advance; a few misfire. "Elegy for a Still-Born Child," for instance, lapses into the kind of ingenuity that mars a number of poems in *Death of a Naturalist*. In this poem a metaphysical conceit based on series of historical, geographical, and astronomical terms—"doomsday," "sphere," "cartographer," "shooting star" and so on—interferes with the elegiac feelings by calling attention to itself as a literary device. But the volume as a whole is a remarkable achievement. "Death of a Naturalist" is a superb poem, the best in the first book, as "A Lough Neagh Sequence" is the best in the second, but the latter poem embraces a whole vision of experience and a wider range of poetic effects. It is a measure of the development from the first to the second collection.

The three final poems in the volume show the poet probing back in time and into the earth in search of underlying forces and the unfathomable, the inscrutable. "Shoreline" evokes the consciousness of history pervading the locale and transcending time: "Take any moment"; "Listen. Is it the Danes,/ A black hawk bent on the sail?/ Or the chinking Normans?" The clay in "Bann Clay" "underruns the valley,/ The first slow residue/ Of a river finding its way." The volume ends with "Bogland," which tells us that "We have no prairies"; "Our pioneers keep striking/ Inwards and downwards"; "The bogholes might be Atlantic seepage./ The wet centre is bottomless." But as Heaney probes inward, and into what lies below and beyond, he does not falsify the physical and emotional actuality of his world. The mythical and mystical do not become unstrung from the earthy or fleshy: the wondrous and the ordinary, the elevated and the colloquial interrelate naturally.

4

Wintering Out

Critical response to Heaney's third volume has been notably ambivalent. Alan Brownjohn in his *New Statesman* review (February 6, 1973), for example, sees a "retrenchment . . . at once baffling and enthralling . . . I both admire *Wintering Out* as one of the best volumes of the last year *and* hope that it represents a mode from which Heaney's remarkable talent will move on." Threading its way through the criticism of Heaney's work is the complaint that despite his indisputable gifts he has restricted his range too severely, and this complaint extends into the commentary on *Wintering Out*. In her review (*Listener*, December 7, 1972) Patricia Beer is restive over his continued exploitation of the regional and rural: "In 'Westering,' . . . written in California, he takes one look at an 'official map of the Moon' and darts straight back to 'the last night/ In Donegal.' "

Some of this reservation is understandable; not all of the poems in this collection reflect the full force of the poet's talent. Indeed, a few are disappointing. The glori-

fication of the road-worker in "Navvy"—"He has not re-
lented/ under weather or insults,/ my brother and
keeper"—is unconvincing, even sentimental. In "Aug-
ury" the sight of a diseased fish becomes the basis for a
direct ecological lament buttressed by rhetorical metaphor, "What . . ./ Can soothe the hurt eye/ Of the sun,"
and a trite figure of decay, "Turn back/ The rat on the
road." Such lapses are the exception.

A larger number of poems illustrate the variety of a
poet who has mastered his technique and is keeping his
options open. "Wedding Day," for instance registers the
humor, tenderness and fears of its emotionally confus-
ing occasion—"When I went to the gents/ There was a
skewered heart/ And a legend of love. Let me/ Sleep on
your breast to the airport." And "Mother of the
Groom" with a sudden focus on the mother's hand af-
fectingly captures not only her aging but the transcend-
ence of her character and the depth of her marital com-
mitment as well—"Once soap would ease off/ The wedding ring/ That's bedded forever now/ In her clapping
hand." Not major poems, these two lead up to one of
the poet's best love poems, "Summer Home," which I
will mention later.

Meanwhile Heaney has retained his adeptness at re-
creating the historical moment, thus continuing the line
of poems from "For the Commander of the 'Eliza'" in
Death of a Naturalist and "Requiem for the Croppies"
in *Door into the Dark*. "Linen Town" with sharp veri-
similitude and the agency of the historical present tense
takes the reader "into" a civic print of High Street,
Belfast, 1786, twelve years before the hanging of the
revolutionist, McCracken. "It's twenty to four," one of

the "last afternoons/ Of reasonable light," and the print "unfreezes" into sensuous reality: "Smell the tidal Lagan:/ Take a last turn/ In the tang of possibility," a graphic detail in the neatly controlled understatement of the poem.

And "The Other Side," which concerns the Catholic-Protestant split, is comparable to the satire of the Paisleyite in "The Docker" in *Death of a Naturalist* but is superior in its balance and emotional complexity to the earlier poem. It unerringly depicts a Protestant neighbor in a satirical characterization that is simultaneously amused, critical, and sympathetic. Adroit, wry, biblical and religious imagery defines the old man as a self-righteous, narrow-minded parody of a patriarch. "He prophesied above our scraggy acres,/ then turned away/ towards his promised furrows"; "His brain was a white-washed kitchen/ hung with texts, swept tidy/ as the body o' the kirk." But he is a pathetic man too: swallowing his pride, shy, trying to act casually, he would come to the door "sometimes when the rosary was dragging/ mournfully on in the kitchen." "But now I stand behind him/ . . .

> Should I slip away, I wonder,
> or go up and touch his shoulder
> and talk about the weather
>
> or the price of grass-seed?

We sense the speaker's humanity in the dilemma; he does very much want to overcome his contempt and separation even if he must resort to banalities of conversation, but what basis for any real communication exists? And that last line sadly and with quiet irony seals the hopelessness.

nights, crossing the thresholds/ Of empty homes, she warmed" herself "in the chimney nook." She is also like a local goddess of spring, of procreation: "She stirred as from a winter/ Sleep. Smiled. Uncradled her breasts." She is then—and how characteristic this is of Heaney's method—simultaneously an actual girl and a spirit of the place, and the poem convinces us of the reality of both manifestations, sensitively, matter-of-factly.

"Maighdean Mara" opens with a dreamy, elegiac but realistically detailed image of what appears to be an actual drowned girl:

> She sleeps now, her cold breasts
> Dandled by undertow,
> Her hair lifted and laid.
> Undulant slow seawracks
> Cast about shin and thigh,
> Bangles of wort, drifting
> Liens catch, dislodge gently.

But the word "sleeps" fuses the real girl with the legend-ary mermaid who must leave the sea and marry the man who steals her magic garment, suffer "man-love nightly/ In earshot of the waves," and "milk and birth," before retrieving her garment and returning to the sea. It is more than a poeticized retelling of the legend; the mer-maid follows an archetypal pattern parallel to entering the cycle of life and its burdens and returning to the source, and the poem accomplishes this without resort-ing to allegory. Corresponding to the human sadness suffered by the mermaid-real girl is the elegiac tone es-tablished at the beginning and maintained to the ending, where the opening two lines are repeated.

Both "Limbo" and "Bye-Child" deal with the searing effects of the shame felt by women who have had illegit-

imate children. The first of these begins with the flat-
ness of a news report: "Fishermen at Ballyshannon/
Netted an infant last night/ Along with the salmon,"
and then moves from seemingly cruel, casual irony but
with an underlying pathos ("An illegitimate spawning,/
A small one thrown back/ To the waters") to the grief
of the mother, "Ducking him tenderly/ Till the frozen
knobs of her wrists/ Were dead as the gravel," the infant
"a minnow with hooks/ Tearing her open." After such
pain what knowledge? Not only that mortal life can
include such an agonizing act but also that in the uni-
verse a region of absolute indifference exists, beyond
even Christ's reach: "Now limbo will be

A cold glitter of souls
Through some far briny zone.
Even Christ's palms, unhealed,
Smart and cannot fish there.

Here, with the transformation of the earlier cold sea
water imagery into that of the cold, stinging "far briny
zone," the ache in the poem reaches a transcendent
level. "Bye-Child" does not achieve quite the profound
chill of "Limbo," but it is painful enough. The boy in
this poem, "Sharp-faced as new moons," "was discovered in the henhouse where she had confined him," an
epigraph, apparently taken from a news item, tells us.
"He was incapable of saying anything." His fate, no less
cruel than that of the infant in "Limbo," is also associated with a cosmic oblivion, for he speaks

With a remote mime
Of something beyond patience,
Your gaping wordless proof
Of lunar distances
Travelled beyond love.

Presenting human loss and alienation within a timeless, archetypal and cosmic perspective, these five poems convey a depth of compassion exceeding that in Heaney's earlier work.

Still, reviewers of *Wintering Out* have been impatient; they want Heaney to "move on" to what they see as more urgent subjects. Two poet-critics would nudge him toward a fuller exploration of the present terror in Ulster. "His poetry expresses deep personal feelings," says Stephen Spender in *The New York Review of Books*, September 20, 1973, "and I suppose it will enlarge to a much wider subject matter, especially since he comes from Northern Ireland, and the Irish situation must be boiling in him." And John Montague in "Order in Donnybrook Fair," an article sorting out Irish poetry (*TLS*, March 17, 1972), offers the opinion, with Heaney in mind, that "the final judgement on the new Ulster Renaissance may well depend on their ability to learn a style from despair: it is the last quarter of the twentieth century we are entering, not the Georgian first." Heaney of course feels the despair of the Irish situation acutely, and he has written poems out of that despair even though he said once in response to a question at a reading that he did not find it obligatory to write poems on the current turmoil in Northern Ireland just because he is a Northern Irish poet: one writes the poems that one must. The dedicatory poem to *Wintering Out* concerns scenes of the nightmarish conflict in Ulster, "the new camp for the internees," a bomb crater, machine-gun posts defining "a real stockade"; "it was déjà-vu, some film made/ of Stalag 17, a bad dream with no sound." The poem ends,

> Is there a life before death? That's chalked up
> on a wall downtown. Competence with pain,
> coherent miseries, a bite and sup,
> we hug our little destiny again.

Although it is not at the center of Heaney's achievement in the volume it casts its numbed despair and futility over what follows. And in one group he brings us back directly to the immediate horror of the Ulster situation.

"A Northern Hoard" (and the homonym horde comes to mind), a five-part sequence, meets with Montague's approval: it is the sort of poem in which the poet's "lost rural childhood and the world in which he now lives begin to come together." He quotes some lines from "Roots," the first of the group, as an example. But I think "Roots" is more problematical than he would have it. It begins with a quiet, stunned lament over the condition that makes love impossible: "In the streetlamp's glow/ Your body's moonstruck/ To drifted barrow, sunk glacial rock"; the style, however, is not entirely successful. Details in the manner of Wilfred Owen and Auden jostle together: "the din/ Of gunshot, siren and clucking gas/ Out there beyond each curtained terrace/ Where the fault is opening." Geological, tree-root, dream, and urban-warfare imagery piles up, becomes clotted as "Roots" moves toward its tormented climax. The speaker will dream the horror, and he performs a necromantic rite:

> I've soaked by moonlight in tidal blood
> A mandrake, lodged human fork,
> Earth sac, limb of the dark;
> And I wound [present tense] its damp smelly loam
> And stop my ears against the scream.

The despair is undeniable but the effect becomes literary, melodramatic, it seems to me.

The three following poems in this sequence are less compacted, shorter, and more effective, although some of the imagery is rather standard in its rhetoric of horror and guilt: "I deserted, shut out/ their wounds' fierce awning [it should be yawning, Heaney tells me] ,/ those palms like streaming webs" ("No Man's Land"). "Tinder" is the last and best poem of the sequence, wherein "We picked flints,/ Pale and dirt-veined"; "What did we know then/ Of tinder, charred linen and iron/ . . .?" In this context a Yeatsian-sounding question takes on more than borrowed force—"What could strike a blaze/ From our dead igneous days?"—and the depiction of savagery at the end is desolating and bitter: "Now we squat on cold cinder,/ . . ./ With new history, flint and iron,/ Cast-offs, scraps, nail, canine." Heaney himself said at a reading that though he thinks he had Paisley in mind the poem, along with being about "the terror behind all," is also about "the unproductive fury" in Ireland—but not limited to Ireland. "A Northern Hoard" is an impressive though not altogether successful attempt to discover a technique adequate to the situation that "must be boiling" in the poet. In "Tinder," however, the anthropological imagery of savagery is closer to the core of Heaney's obsessions, his concern with a primal consciousness.

As I have indicated, critical response has so far evinced some resistance to Heaney's central preoccupations, has tended to miss the point that his unique qualities derive from his determination to follow his own unmodish impulses. In one sense this means to be a traditional Irish poet. As Denis Donoghue says in "The problems of being Irish," which he wrote for a special Irish issue of the *Times Literary Supplement* (March 17, 1972), the "best writers in Ireland are those who have remembered most. . . I mean those writers who feel immediate experience not merely in itself but in relation to a grand perspective which is likely to be mythological and historical, pagan and Christian." In another sense this may mean that, paradoxically, he is very current, so unmodish that he has struck on one clearly emerging contemporary concern. Bernardo Bertolucci, the filmmaker, speaking from a Marxist point of view and rather romantically, says in a recent *Guardian* interview that he wants to carry the younger generations "back to the rediscovery of their real roots which are those of the peasant world. I want to carry the camera into the cornfields, into the furrows of earth during irrigation, into the ground itself"; he speaks of "the great mass who . . . are perfectly ignorant of their own roots . . . I just don't believe that a few decades can cancel out generations of genetic memory . . . there must be a memory of the values of the land." In either case my contention is that the matter and method of the poetry cut through notions of its limited range or lack of timeliness. By its explorations of a historical and pagan mythos, by its concern for the land and for cultural roots, and by its inward searchings it overcomes mere traditionalism or Irish provincialism and assumes a depth and impact available to us if we do not insist that it conform to another mode.

Wintering Out opens on a note of nostalgia. The speaker in "Fodder" ("Or, as we said,/ *fother*") yearns for the prelapsarian blessings of hay, which he enjoyed as a boy, "swathes of grass/ and meadowsweet/ multiple as loaves/ and fishes." Openly nostalgic, he is not indulgently so, for his yearning arises from his current adult restlessness and frustration: "These long nights/ I would pull hay/ for comfort, anything/ to bed the stall." This is not a profound statement, but it draws the reader into a tracing of roots deeper and more extensive than the personal ones of childhood. The first five poems could in fact be subheaded "The Backward Look," to use the title of a later poem in the book. In his *Guardian* essay, discussing why he feels at a remove from Spenser, Heaney says, "From his castle in Cork he watched the effects of a campaign designed to settle the Irish question. 'Out of every corner of the woods and glens they came creeping forth upon their hands, for their legs could not carry them; they looked like anatomies of death . . .' At that point I feel closer to the natives, the geniuses of the place," and I believe that Heaney must have in mind the Latin root meanings of genius: a guardian deity or spirit of a person, spirit. His statement with its quotation from Spenser is a fine gloss on "Bog Oak," in which a seasoned black rib of bog oak under the thatch stirs the speaker to reflect, "I might tarry/ with the moustached dead," "or eavesdrop on/ their hopeless wisdom," but his brooding lament over the fate of these geniuses leads to bitter irony and a deepening of the lament as he envisions Spenser "dreaming sunlight, encroached upon by/ geniuses who creep/ . . ./ towards watercress and carrion," desperate, terribly abused men who were nevertheless in touch with the life cycle, as suggested by "watercress and carrion"—a part of their "hopeless wisdom."

Other manifestations of these geniuses appear in "Servant Boy" and "The Last Mummer." The servant boy, "Old work-whore, slave-/ blood," to members of the

Ascendancy presumably, "is wintering out"—the present tense imparts a legendary character to him—"the back-end of a bad year," but his spirit is not quashed. "First-footing/ the back doors of the little barons," he comes "resentful/ and impenitent,/ carrying the warm eggs," carrying, that is, the tradition he represents live and intact, carrying too the symbols of regenerative power, warm within the coldness of winter, and the capacity for survival. "How/ you draw me into your trail," says the speaker addressing the boy, and Heaney's desire to identify with the boy is evident in his choosing the phrase from this poem for the book's title. The last mummer is also at least partly an impenitent bearer of ancient Irish tradition, whose "straw mask and hunch were fabulous," but in the contemporary world he is out of place, reduced to a figure who "Moves out of the fog/ on the lawn, pads up the terrace" (of a manor house?) where a "luminous screen" (for films? a TV set?) has people "charmed in a ring," not at all aware that the mummer's traditional roles, "St. George, Beel-zebub and Jack Straw," cannot "be conjured from such mist." Bitter and frustrated, he hurls a stone upon the slates of the roof as he departs. His rage may be related to the fact that Heaney said once when introducing the poem that it "could be about Paisley," suggesting, I think, the perversion and degeneration of the traditional values into hatred and violence. But he also said that it "could be about poetry," and in the final section the mummer is evoked in his original role: he is a poetic spirit "who had/ untousled a first dewy path/ into the summer grazing"—the world of nature and myth.

A mood of trance, of dreamlike recall, suffuses these

poems but their beings emerge as living presences. And
so too with "Anahorish," which, however, opens up another dimension. This poem, like "Fodder," refers back
to a prelapsarian condition: "My 'place of clear water'
[the meaning of Anahorish],/ the first hill in the world/
where springs washed into/ the shiny grass." The very
sound of the townland's name, its music, summons up
an "after-image of lamps/ swung through the yards/ on
winter evenings," and the inhabitants included in that
image are presences who go (again the present tense)
"Waistdeep in mist/ to break the light ice/ at wells and
dunghills." They are "mound-dwellers," and this anthropological term suggests a human continuity, a genetic
memory. It is this sense of continuity and the sense of
identity with our remote forebears which Heaney conveys with such intensity and poignance in "The Tollund
Man," further on in *Wintering Out*.

This poem calls to mind the appropriateness of Michel
Benamou's assertation in his *Wallace Stevens and the
Symbolist Imagination*, "Poets and anthropologists
share the same nostalgia for origins, for a center";
Heaney's "backward look" for origins, for identities, is
certainly informed by an anthropological imagination.
"The Tollund Man" and "Nerthus," a companion poem,
derive in fact from the poet's reading of P. V. Glob's
The Bog People. The Tollund Man was a spirit of his
place, chosen as "Bridegroom to the goddess" in a ritual
assuring the revival of spring each year, then sacrificed
by her: "She tightened her torc on him" (the word torc
working with a double force), and "Those dark juices"
worked him "to a saint's kept body." At the same time
the speaker would have this saint restore, redeem, sanc-

tify the slaughtered Irish, the "Stockinged corpses/ Laid out in the farmyards." To appreciate this poem it is unnecessary to read *The Bog People*; the poet presents what is essential to his purpose. To look at the photographs in Glob's book, though, is to realize how accurately the poet renders the bog man, dug out of the "Trove of the turfcutters'/ Honeycombed workings."

> Some day I will go to Aarhus
> To see his peat-brown head,
> The mild pods of his eye-lids,
> His pointed skin cap.

Accurate but, moreover, gently reverent, especially in the delicacy of word and sound in the third line. The preserved human body becomes a symbol of the pain and pathos of man's condition, a saint worthy of the pilgrimage the speaker desires to make someday. It does not seem, therefore, that the speaker is extravagant when he exclaims,

> I could risk blasphemy,
> Consecrate the cauldron bog
> Our holy ground and pray
> Him to make germinate
>
> The scattered, ambushed
> Flesh of labourers, . . .

The rhetoric is reminiscent of Dylan Thomas's; and Patricia Beer does detect a few lines in *Wintering Out* that echo Thomas. But as she says, and I believe for the most part rightly, "His poems do remind of us of someone but it always turns out to be Seamus Heaney." The speaker wishes for "Something of his sad freedom/ As he rode the tumbril" to his death, "Naked except for/ The cap, noose and girdle," and he concludes,

Out there in Jutland
In the old man-killing parishes
I will feel lost,
Unhappy and at home.

For John Montague "the violence of the 'old man-killing parishes' is seen as part of whole Nordic ritual," but for me it encompasses a more universal significance than this suggests—beyond Denmark, beyond Ireland. In the Tollund Man Heaney has found a symbol of the timeless forces of separation, death and resurrection with which he can identify. As Heaney said at that same reading I have referred to, "the bog preserves not only bodies but also consciousness."

Alfred Kazin in *Bright Book of Life* claims that "Man's immortality, if he can be said to have one at all, reaches into the past, not into the future: It lies in a candid sense of history, not in the hope offered by orthodox Christianity." A complementary view as expressed by George Moore in *Hail and Farewell* is that "paganism is primordial fire, and it is always breaking through the Christian crust." Heaney's Christianity may be firmer than Moore would allow, but he is surely "at home" with the pagan and the primordial. His profound sympathy and respect for pagan holiness—and I would surmise that he would feel that Christianity has subsumed it—is evident in "Nerthus" (a goddess of the Bog People, who worshipped her with elongated, austerely carved, almost abstract icons):

For beauty, say an ash-fork staked in peat,
Its long grains gathering to the gouged split;

A seasoned, unsleeved taker of the weather,
Where kesh and loaning finger out to heather.

This is the complete poem, brief to the point of being
laconic, but lyrically affecting, with the Northern dia-
lect words "kesh" (causeway) and "loaning" (a space
between uncultivated fields) stressing the primitive isolation. These icons also wintered out. "It is easy," says
Michel Benamou, "to succumb . . . to . . . the anthropological temptation," to be caught in a "nostalgic circle."
This is the sort of issue on which judgment of the poet's
work ought to pivot, not on such questions as whether
or not his subject matter is limited. In "Nerthus" and
"The Tollund Man," it seems to me, the accuracy of
physical detail and the governing tone of austere nobility cancel thoughts of nostalgia or of sentimentality.
Only in "May" does Heaney's desire for the primitive
lead him into that nostalgic circle: "I should wear/ Hide
shoes, the hair next my skin,/ For walking this ground,"
"the soft fontanel/ Of Ireland."

It remains to consider one final group of poems in
Wintering Out. In these Heaney concentrates on two
further subjects which fascinate him, man's relationship
with the land, with nature, and a corollary subject, as it
turns out, language. Bertolucci would, as he said, take
his camera right *into* the earth; Heaney in effect extracts
the language of his poetry *from* the earth. The subject
of "Oracle," a short and initially enigmatic poem, is
inseparably part of nature. Whom is the speaker addressing when he advises, "Hide in the hollow trunk/ of the
willow tree,/ . . ./ until, as usual, they/ cuckoo your
name/ across the fields"? And who are "they"? They, it
seems, are simply grownups coming after a hiding child,
but the child is also symbolically an oracle who has an
instinctual, animal-like identity with nature, who is in-

deed yet another genius of the place: an air of mystery
and wonder pervades the poem and the speaker refers to
him as "small mouth and ear/ in a woody cleft,/ lobe
and larynx/ of the mossy places." The child, finally,
appears to be the incipient poet, taking in the sounds of
nature and transmitting them.

"Land" also develops the theme of identity with
nature but is at the same time a prescription for a man
who would live in accord with the values derived from
that identity. The speaker "composed habits for those
acres/ so that my last look would be/ neither gluttonous
nor starved." Like Eliot's Fisher King, he would set his
lands in order. He raised a small cairn, and out of his
reverence for the land he would leave part of it "plaited
and branchy" while erecting "a woman of old wet
leaves,/ rush-bands and thatcher's scollops,/ stooked
loosely"; she would be in effect a symbolic fertility goddess, "her breasts an open-work/ of new straw and har-
vest bows"; she would gaze "out past/ the shifting
hares." Unlike Eliot he insists on a more than symbolic
physical closeness to the land, and in the last section he
speaks in the present tense, in lines that may remind one
of Roethke, though he makes them his own (by this
time Heaney had written a sympathetic review of the
American poet's work): "I sense the pads [the hares'
footprints or tracks evidently]/ unfurling under grass
and clover"; he enters the world of the hares, other spir-
its of the place, who inhabit the "phantom ground."
The speaker's affinity with the hares includes an awareness that he too might find himself "snared, swinging/
an ear-ring of sharp wire." This recognition of his poten-
tial sudden death is part of his consciousness, which in

turn is part of his total relation with the land; his awareness encompasses both the animal and the human as-
pects of earth, in balance.

The speaker is like the mammal in "Gifts of Rain"
who senses "weather by his skin" and "fords/ his life by
sounding./ Soundings." The rains are a blessing; flooded
fields become "an atlantis" a man "depends on," and
the man described is part of an image that conveys harmony, purpose, and order: "he is hooped to where he
planted/ and sky and ground/ are running naturally
among his arms/ that grope the cropping land." Dives
(popular name for the rich man in the parable, Luke
16:19-31) is the speaker in this poem, and in this case a
man rich in his sensitive awareness both of nature's blessings and of its ruinous power. He responds to the abun-
dance of the flooding and its exciting beautiful music
but feels the "need/ for antediluvian lore" (the last
phrase catching well one of Heaney's own obsessions).
And he hears "Soft voices of the dead/ . . ./ whispering
by the shore"; he would question them "(and for my
children's sake)/ about crops rotted, river mud/ glazing
the baked clay floor," for knowledge of the famine and
the destructive force of the flooding should not be
erased from consciousness. It too is part of the continuity, the tradition, the genetic memory, that must be
passed on.

Jon Silkin in his fine essay "Bedding the Locale" in
New Blackfriars (March, 1973) cites the accuracy of
these lines in "Gifts of Rain,"

> a flower of mud-
> water blooms up to his reflection
>
> like a cut swaying
> its red spores through a basin.

Here, he says, is "a fusing of the traditional concerns of
the land with the modern analytic image, held finally
together by 'spores,' and which occurs in the contrasted
perception of the *domestic* water safely contained by
the wash-basin"; the images "fuse together two different
consciousnesses, without strain or deftness. Here one
notes the real advance in Heaney's work." It is one advance, but there is another to which Silkin gives passing
attention. The swollen Moyola river in "Gifts of Rain"
is "an old chanter," "bedding the locale/ in the utterance," is music "breathing its mists/ through vowels and
history." Bedding the locale in the utterance is an appropriate phrase for a considerable number of poems in
Wintering Out. Language is one more genius of the
place; its roots are in natural sounds and in the native
tradition, the Gaelic word often indeed a transliteration
of nature's ur-language—"*Anahorish,* soft gradient/ of
consonant, vowel-meadow"; the river in "Toome" says
of itself, "My mouth holds round/ the soft blastings,/
Toome, Toome"; in "Broagh" (which means riverbank)
the sounds of the name are associated with the rain, so
that a shower's "low tattoo/ among the windy boor-
trees/ and rhubarb-blades/ ended almost/ suddenly, like
the last/ *gh* the strangers found/ difficult to manage,"
and here both the natural origins of the word and its
native integrity are accented by the knowing humor.
These are just a few of many such examples.

Patricia Beer says, "Heaney is not only concerned
with sound but obsessed with pronunciation: in poem
after poem, vowels, consonants, the organs of speech
themselves provide metaphor," but in a short review she
did not have space to develop her point, a point which
nevertheless reflects how seriously the poet means his
statement to me that "the seeds were in language,

words." In *Death of a Naturalist* "Saint Francis and the Birds" treats his obsession with language in a relatively superficial and conventional way, as the birds to which the saint has preached love "throttled up/ Into the blue like a flock of words," "Which was the best poem Francis made./ His argument true, his tone light." This is pleasant enough with its play on words-birds, but it does not begin to plumb what Heaney has called the "subconscious and semantic energies of words." The word-play in the poems just discussed is exuberant, extravagant; in fact, in one instance at least, "A New Song," he carries himself away on a flood of river-linguistic-political metaphor:

> But now our river tongues must rise
> From licking deep in native haunts
> To flood, with vowelling embrace,
> Demesnes staked out in consonants.
>
> And Castledawson we'll enlist
> And Upperlands, each planted bawn—

Even this excess reveals his delight in discovering the source of verbal energies. Moreover, this third volume makes overt what has been implicit in his method. I said earlier in this study that it is difficult to draw a clear line in Heaney's work separating poetic artifice and physical reality, that two become one in the body of the poem. What this means finally is that Heaney sees language as a process of transubstantiation: nature, experience, feelings incarnate in the word, in the texture of the poem. When the speaker finds himself out "On a scurf of winkles and cockles" in "Dawn," "Unable to move without crunching/ Acres of their crisp delicate turrets," the phrasing and prosody seem to *embody* the brittle vulnerability of those shells.

With poetic form Heaney has not been obviously experimental, although from the start he has been flexible about rhyme, often in the most set forms using occasional and slant rhyme, often dispensing with it altogether while employing vowel and consonant clusters for an aural concreteness more integrally part of a poem's effect than a rhyme-scheme. In *Wintering Out* rhyme is much less evident, and the rhythms tend to be more fluid, without a loss of concreteness. And, as a number of poems in the last two books show, he has not shunned free-verse when it suited his needs. That is, he has headed toward a more open poetry while generally retaining a stanzaic framework. His future work may be yet more radical in form, but who is to predict?

I like to think that "Summer Home," one of his best love poems, represents one possible line of development. This poem, with very personal intonations, examines the skein of guilt, love, and atonement that binds a husband and wife. It is in five sections with links that are not at once apparent so that the significance of each section wells up, sometimes obliquely, as we read. The lovers' "wound" is anointed, atoned for, bodily—"with a final/ unmusical drive/ long grains begin to split"—and reverently—"as you bend in the shower/ water lives down the tilting stoups of your breasts"—and the technical religious word "stoups," which sounds unpoetic, is wonderfully apt as the stone basin for holy water becomes visible flesh. Here is the first section, in which the speaker seems to be returning home laden with unspecified sexual guilt:

> Was it wind off the dumps
> Or something in heat
>
> dogging us, the summer gone sour,
> a fouled nest incubating somewhere?
>
> Whose fault, I wondered, inquisitor
> of the possessed air.
>
> To realize suddenly,
> whip off the mat
>
> that was larval, moving—
> and scald, scald, scald.

The lines, puzzled, probing, and at the end explosive,
move naturally in the rhythms of live speech. They convey not only the oppressiveness of the rancid air but
also, in "something in heat/ dogging us" and "a fouled
nest incubating somewhere," a sense of perverse, soured
sexuality, thereby lending an immediacy to what must
be a displacement of the speaker's own anxieties over "a
summer gone sour." Thus in scalding the maggoty door-
mat, the source of the corrupt odor, he seems to be
performing an intense symbolic ritual of self-purgation.
An intense poem, it characterizes the poet's subtle mod-
ulation in *Wintering Out* toward freer movement and
more open form.

Wintering Out is part of a development that extends
through the three volumes, but it is also a culmination, a
fulfillment: what began with the early shocks of recognition in *Death of a Naturalist* has evolved by the third
book into a mature vision which derives from what the
poet has referred to as the "dark centre, the blurred and
irrational storehouse of insight and instincts, the hidden

core of the self" and which is related intimately to the
land and to his heritage. Such thoughts were perhaps in
Heaney's mind when he said to me that he feels the first
three books amount to a completed opus. This naturally
raises the question of where he might go from here, but
I think we can only wait patiently for whatever develop-
ments lie in store.

One thing we can definitely expect in the near future
is a translation of the *Buile Shuibhne*, the Middle Irish
romance which the poet has been working on. I have
read several passages of his translation and must say it
appears to be a work most congenial to his talents. Here
for example are three stanzas from a poem spoken by
the mythical figure Sweeney when driven to a mad despair, suffering the hardship of snow and cold:

Then after this snow, a wind
stropped on the frost,
scourged trees that cry in me
for the brink of winter.

Branches smithied in ice
have opened me,
the briars' crimson streamer
was the skin of my feet

and the frostbite in my fingers
has put me astray—
from Slieve Mish to Cullion,
from Cullion to Cooley.

This translation should take its place alongside Thomas
Kinsella's translation of *The Tain*, adding to the body
of excellent modern translation of early Irish literature
being done in Ireland. Meanwhile Heaney continues to
write his own poetry, carrying on his essential contribution to the flourishing state of Irish poetry today. For

all its native authenticity, however, his is not an insular
poetry. Seamus Heaney's best poems define their land-
scape and human experience with such visceral clarity,
immediacy, and integrity of feeling that they transcend
their regional source and make a significant contribution
to contemporary poetry written in English.

Select Bibliography

TEXTS

Death of a Naturalist. London: Faber and Faber, 1966.
Door into the Dark. London: Faber and Faber, 1969.
Wintering Out. London: Faber and Faber, 1972.

HEANEY'S PROSE

"Canticles to the Earth." A review of *The Collected Poems of Theodore Roethke*. *The Listener* (August 22, 1968), pp. 245-46. *The Listener* and *New Statesman* have published other reviews and short essays by Heaney (including several of an autobiographical nature) too numerous to cite here.
"The Trade of an Irish Poet." *The Guardian* (May 25, 1972), p. 17.
"Deep as England." A review of *Selected Poems* by Ted Hughes. *Hibernia* (December 1, 1972), p. 13.

ARTICLES AND REVIEWS

Beer, Patricia. "Seamus Heaney's Third Book of Poems." *The Listener* (December 7, 1972), p. 795.
Kiely, Benedict. "A Raid into Dark Corners: the Poems of Seamus Heaney." *The Hollins Critic* 7 (October 4, 1970): 1-12.
Longley, Michael. "Poetry," in Michael Longley, ed, *Causeway: the Arts in Ulster* (Arts Council of Northern Ireland, Belfast, 1971). See pp. 106-7.

Montague, John. "Order in Donnybrook Fair." *TLS* (March 17, 1972), p. 313.

Press, John. "Ted Walker, Seamus Heaney, and Kenneth White: Three New Poets." *Southern Review* 5 (Summer 1969): 673-88.

Silkin, Jon. "Bedding the Locale." *New Blackfriars* 54 (March 1973): 130-33.